Date: 11/19/21

J 796.323 PRY
Pryor, Shawn,
Basketball's most
ridonkulous dunks! /

D1502386

Prime Time Plays

BASKETBALL'S MOST RIDONKULOUS DUNKS!

by Shawn Pryor

CAPSTONE PRESS
a capstone imprint

Capstone Captivate is published by Capstone Press, an imprint of Capstone.
1710 Roe Crest Drive, North Mankato, Minnesota 56003
www.capstonepub.com

SPORTS ILLUSTRATED KIDS is a trademark of ABG-SI LLC. Used with
permission.

Library of Congress Cataloging-in-Publication Data
Names: Pryor, Shawn, author.
Title: Basketball's most ridonkulous dunks! / by Shawn Pryor.
Description: North Mankato, Minnesota : Capstone Press, 2021. | Series: Sports
    illustrated kids prime time plays | Includes index. | Audience: Ages 8-11 | Audience:
    Grades 4-6 | Summary: "Whoosh! When the high-tops leave the hardwood, it's
    prime time on the basketball court. From monster in-game jams to gravity-defying
    contest slams, experience the most ridonkulous dunks from pro basketball's
    biggest superstars. Some of these rim-rocking plays even blew out the
    backboards!"—Provided by publisher.
Identifiers: LCCN 2020025101 (print) | LCCN 2020025102 (ebook) | ISBN
    9781496695338 (library binding) | ISBN 9781496696885 (paperback) |
    ISBN 9781977153852 (pdf)
Subjects: LCSH: Basketball—History—Juvenile literature. | Dunking (Basketball)—
    Juvenile literature.
Classification: LCC GV885.1 .P79 2021 (print) | LCC GV885.1 (ebook) | DDC
    796.323—dc23
LC record available at https://lccn.loc.gov/2020025101
LC ebook record available at https://lccn.loc.gov/2020025102

Image Credits
AP Images: ASSOCIATED PRESS, 7, Craig Mitchelldyer, 13, Eric Christian Smith,
21, Mark Blinch, 28, Ross D. Franklin, 19; Dreamstime: Jerry Coli, 10, Laurence
Agron, 6; Getty Images: Darren McNamara, 17, Steve Russell, 29; Newscom: David
T. Foster III/TNS, 23, JEFF HAYNES, 27, Jon SooHoo/UPI/, 15; Shutterstock: Alex
Kravtsov, Cover, BK_graphic, (geometric) design elements; Sports Illustrated: Andy
Hayt, 11, top 25, bottom 25, John W. McDonough, 5, 14, 16, Manny Millan, 9, 26,
Walter Iooss Jr, 8

Editorial Credits
Editor: Christopher Harbo; Designer: Sarah Bennett; Media Researcher: Eric Gohl;
Production Specialist: Katy LaVigne

Printed and bound in the USA. PO 3837

TABLE OF CONTENTS

Words in **bold** are in the glossary.

DYNAMIC DUNKS

Eight seconds remain, and the game is tied. The man-to-man **defense** has the **offense** locked up when the point guard sees his power forward set a pick. The point guard swerves left around the defender and charges the open **lane**. As he nears the basket, he takes flight, swirls his arm like a windmill, and delivers a dynamic dunk. The game is over, and the crowd goes wild!

The slam dunk is one of the most exciting plays in the National Basketball Association (NBA). It's loaded with action, power, and lots of air! From the power dunkers of the past to today's superstars, this book has the mega jams and monster slams you love. Get ready to see the players and moments that left people screaming for more. These are basketball's most ridonkulous dunks!

Everyone on the court looks on in awe as Dwyane Wade of the Miami Heat throws down a powerful slam dunk during the 2012 NBA Finals.

CHAPTER 1

LEGENDARY JAMMERS

Slam dunks are a huge part of the game—but they weren't always that way. Here are some of the legendary jammers who made dunking the showstopper it is today.

Thunderous Dunks

In 1975, Darryl Dawkins became the first player to enter the NBA **draft** right out of high school. At 6 feet, 11 inches (211 centimeters) tall, his strength and size made him famous for defense and hard **fouls**. But everyone feared his powerful dunks most of all.

Darryl Dawkins dunks over the head of Kent Benson of the Milwaukee Bucks in 1979.

What made Dawkins a monster dunker?
His hands sometimes hit the rim with such force
during two-handed jams that he shattered the glass
backboard! Playing for the Philadelphia 76ers in 1979,
he destroyed backboards twice. The first was during a
game against the Kansas City Kings on November 13.
The second came just three weeks later against the
San Antonio Spurs.

A shower of glass rains down on players after Dawkins slam dunks the ball against the San Antonio Spurs in 1979.

Rock the Baby

Julius "Dr. J" Erving of the Philadelphia 76ers was one of the original high-flying dunk masters. In fact, he was the first player to dunk a ball after taking off from the free-throw line in an NBA slam-dunk contest. But one of Dr. J's most famous dunks came in a game against the Los Angeles Lakers in 1983.

Julius "Dr. J" Erving

When a tipped pass led to a loose ball, Dr. J snatched it up and took off on a breakaway. Lakers guard Michael Cooper hustled back to defend, but Erving jumped high over him. On his way up, Dr. J cradled the ball in his right hand and rocked his arm back and forth. Then he swooped his arm and jammed the ball home. A **broadcaster** said Erving "rocked the baby" on his way up for the dunk. That's how one of basketball's most famous dunks earned its name.

Dr. J commands the court as he dunks the ball against the Los Angeles Lakers in the 1982 NBA Finals.

Double Pump Dunker

Dominique Wilkins was nicknamed "The Human Highlight Film" for good reason. The high-flying Atlanta Hawks forward was one of the most dynamic dunkers of all time. His "double-pump" slam dunks were a mixture of grace and power.

During his **rookie** season in 1982, Wilkins put on a show every night he touched the floor. In a game on November 12 against the Utah Jazz, Atlanta guard Rory Sparrow stole the ball and led a fast break on offense. Wilkins quickly trailed behind him as the Jazz rushed to play defense. As Sparrow got close to the basket, he passed the ball backward. Wilkins grabbed it, leaped, and smashed the double-pump dunk home—all while being fouled!

Dominique Wilkins

> **FACT**
>
> Wilkins took part in five slam-dunk contests, winning two, in 1985 and in 1990.

Dominique Wilkins jams a two-handed reverse slam through the hoop during the 1987 NBA All-Star Game.

CHAPTER 2

MODERN-ERA MARVELS

Today's NBA modern-era marvels have given us many highlights over the years. Here are the future Hall-of-Famers and lifetime playmakers who have given us the most spectacular super-dunks.

Slam Jam

LeBron James has spent many seasons wowing fans with his high-flying highlights. When it comes to dunking, the multiple league champion has proven he's one of the best. But when James switched teams to the Los Angeles Lakers in 2018, he didn't waste any time showing that he still had something to prove.

During the season opener against the Portland Trail Blazers, the Lakers grabbed a quick lead. Then, just three minutes into the game, James put on a show. Taking an **inbound** pass from Rajon Rondo, James dribbled up court. Slicing through defenders, he crossed center court and took the open lane. With a mighty leap, he wound his arm back and slammed the ball through the hoop! The crowd went wild, and James became a hero to his new Lakers fans!

LeBron James makes his mark as a Los Angeles Laker with a powerful dunk in the first game of the 2018 season against the Portland Trail Blazers.

Stuff of a Legend

During his legendary career, Lakers star Kobe Bryant had more than his fair share of stunning dunks. But by the 2014–15 season, many people wondered if he had anything left in the tank. Some thought he had lost a step and it was time to retire. Little did they know, Bryant was about to prove them wrong.

In the third game of the Lakers' 2014 season, the Los Angeles Clippers jumped out to an early lead. But Bryant wasn't about to let the Clippers get comfortable. About halfway through the first quarter, Jeremy Lin bounced him a pass. Bryant swung around defender Matt Barnes and took the ball to the basket. With a 180-degree power slam, Bryant swiftly silenced anyone who doubted his greatness!

FACT

In December 2014, Bryant passed Michael Jordan as the NBA's third-leading all-time scorer. He has since fallen to number four, behind LeBron James.

Kobe Bryant rises to the rim to complete his 180-degree power slam against Matt Barnes of the Los Angeles Clippers.

The Dunk of Death

In 2000, Vince Carter was an up-and-coming superstar with the Toronto Raptors. The strong defender was a scoring machine and a slam-dunk **specialist**. Nowhere did Carter's dunking ability shine more than as a member of Team USA in the 2000 Summer Olympics.

The Elbow Dunk

In 2000, Carter performed his famous "Elbow Dunk" during the NBA All-Star slam-dunk contest. The stunning dunk ended with Carter hanging from the rim by his elbow! Ouch!

In a game against Team France, Carter stole a fast-break pass and drove down the lane. Between him and the basket stood 7-foot-2-inch- (218-cm-) tall center Frédéric Weis. Would Carter go around this towering giant? No way! The NBA star leaped clear over Weis' head and jammed the ball home. The amazing dunk shocked both Weis and the crowd. It soon became known simply as "The Dunk of Death."

Vince Carter leaps clear over the head of Team France center Frédéric Weis to complete one of the most famous dunks in Olympics history.

CHAPTER 3

NEW FREQUENT FLYERS

The slam dunk has definitely evolved over the years. To see what the future of dunking in the NBA will be like, look no further than these new frequent flyers.

Power-Dunk Pro

Ja Morant joined the NBA in 2019, and the explosive guard made a name for himself right away. In just his first season, the rookie was a highlight-making machine for the Memphis Grizzlies. One such golden moment came with a stunning dunk on December 11 against the Phoenix Suns.

The Grizzlies were clinging to a four-point lead with only a minute left. One wrong move and the Suns would be back in the game. But Morant wasn't going to let that happen. Taking the inbound pass, he dribbled up court. A quick pick-and-roll left Suns center Aron Baynes to guard the feisty rookie. Baynes pushed Morant out to the three-point line, then Morant pushed back and took the ball to the hoop. Baynes followed, but Morant jumped over him to slam a power dunk that all but put the game away.

Ja Morant powers past Phoenix Suns center Aron Baynes to put the ball—and the game—away with a decisive dunk.

King of Clutch

Utah Jazz forward Donovan Mitchell is another young superstar who knows how to make clutch plays. He's one of the reasons why the Jazz have been such a strong team in the Western Conference. He also knows how to pull off timely dunks when his team needs them most!

During Game 2 of the 2018 Western Conference Semifinals, the Jazz were playing a tough Houston Rockets team. Mitchell was being guarded fiercely by Trevor Ariza. As Mitchell charged the basket, Ariza's block made Mitchell shuffle his feet. To keep himself from **traveling**, Mitchell took a quick shot. As the ball bounced off the rim, Mitchell leaped over three Rockets, grabbed the ball, and jammed it through the hoop. This stuff put the Jazz back in the lead!

FACT

In 2018, Donovan Mitchell placed second in Rookie of the Year voting behind Ben Simmons of the Philadelphia 76ers.

Donovan Mitchell hangs from the rim after his incredible jam against the Houston Rockets in Game 2 of the 2018 Western Conference Semifinals.

Amazing Antetokounmpo

Milwaukee Bucks star Giannis Antetokounmpo can do it all on the basketball court. Need a bucket? Give the ball to Antetokounmpo. Need a defender on your opponent's top scorer? Let Antetokounmpo guard him. Need a super-dunk highlight for the world to see? Go get Antetokounmpo!

The 2019 All-Star Game was filled with incredible plays. But one of the best plays of the game was a dunk by Antetokounmpo. On a fast break, Stephen Curry made a high bounce pass toward the basket. The ball bounced so high that it looked like it was going to go over the backboard. Without missing a beat, Antetokounmpo jumped skyward, grabbed the ball above the rim, and slammed it in. The crowd went bonkers!

Giannis Antetokounmpo's face lights up with pure joy as he stuffs the ball through the hoop during the 2019 All-Star Game.

CHAPTER 4

SLAM-DUNK CONTEST SUPERSTARS

The NBA slam-dunk contest is the crown jewel of every All-Star break. Here are some of the contest's brightest-shining superstars!

Air Jordan

Michael Jordan wasn't called Air Jordan by accident. With a ball in his hand and an opening to the basket, Jordan could practically fly. And nowhere were his skills on display more than in the 1987 slam-dunk contest.

During the event, Jordan pulled off one amazing slam after another. He did Dr. J's Rock the Baby dunk. He also showed off his own Kiss the Rim dunk, where his head was so close to the rim he could have kissed it. But the Chicago Bulls superstar truly took flight with his Free-Throw Line dunk. After lifting off from the free-throw line, he soared through the air. Flashbulbs popped as cameras snapped one of the most **iconic** dunks in basketball history.

Michael Jordan spins and ducks under the basket to wow the crowd with a stunning slam dunk during the 1987 slam-dunk contest.

Jordan soars through the air after leaping from the free-throw line to complete one of the most famous dunks in the history of the slam-dunk contest.

Superman Soars

By 2008, Dwight Howard was already a three-time NBA All-Star in five seasons with the Orlando Magic. The master of **rebounding**, defense, and scoring points also loved superheroes. To show it, he pulled off something truly super in the 2008 slam-dunk contest.

Mighty Spud

Just 5 feet, 6 inches (168 cm) tall, Spud Webb played guard for the Atlanta Hawks. In 1986, he defied his size and gravity in the slam-dunk contest. With his amazing leaping ability, he won the contest, and today he remains the shortest player ever to do so.

Spud Webb shows off his remarkable leaping ability next to the much taller Manute Bol.

Before one of his dunks, Howard took off his Magic jersey to reveal a Superman T-shirt. Then a teammate tied a cape around his neck, and Howard stepped to the half-court line. As Howard ran toward the basket, his teammate, Jameer Nelson, tossed the ball in an arching **alley-oop**. Just in front of the free-throw line, Howard leaped. As his cape fluttered behind him, he caught the ball and soared toward the basket. Extending his arm, Howard slammed the ball through the hoop for a super-dunk!

Dwight Howard's cape flutters behind him as he delivers a super-powered slam during the 2008 dunk contest.

The Mascot Dunk

Orlando Magic star Aaron Gordon has competed in several NBA slam-dunk contests. Although he has yet to win one, Gordon has put on a show every time he has competed. One of his most stunning dunks came in 2016. He and Zach LaVine of the Minnesota Timberwolves were going back and forth every single round.

Slam-Dunk Contest Winners Since 2010

2010—Nate Robinson, New York Knicks

2011—Blake Griffin, LA Clippers

2012—Jeremy Evans , Utah Jazz

2013—Terrence Ross, Toronto Raptors

2014—John Wall, Washington Wizards

2015—Zach LaVine, Minnesota
Timberwolves

2016—Zach LaVine, Minnesota
Timberwolves

2017—Glenn Robinson III, Indiana
Pacers

2018—Donovan Mitchell, Utah Jazz

2019—Hamidou Diallo, Oklahoma
City Thunder

2020—Derrick Jones Jr., Miami Heat

Zack LaVine in 2016

Gordon knew he had to do something to one-up LaVine. So he asked the Orlando Magic **mascot** to stand near the basket and hold a basketball over its head. Then Gordon walked to the three-point line. Turning, he ran toward the mascot and leaped! As he passed over the mascot's head, Gordon grabbed the ball, passed it under both legs, and smashed it through the hoop. What a dunk!

Aaron Gordon defies gravity to glide over the head of Stuff the Magic Dragon during the 2016 slam-dunk contest.

GLOSSARY

alley-oop (AL-ee-oop)—a move in which a player throws a ball so another player can leap up near the basket to catch it and make a basket, usually a dunk, in one motion

broadcaster (BRAHD-kast-uhr)—a person who calls play-by-play on the TV or radio during a sporting event

defense (di-FENSS)—the team that tries to stop points from being scored

draft (DRAFT)—an event in which athletes are picked to join sports organizations or teams

foul (FOUL)—an action in basketball that is against the rules

iconic (EYE-cahn-ik)—widely viewed as perfectly capturing the meaning or spirit of something or someone

inbound (IN-bound)—thrown into play from out-of-bounds

lane (LAYN)—the rectangle-shaped area in front of the basket

mascot (MASS-kot)—a person or animal that represents a sports team

offense (aw-FENSS)—the team that is in control of the ball and is trying to score

rebound (REE-bound)—the act of gaining possession of the ball after a missed shot

rookie (RUK-ee)—a first-year player

specialist (SPESH-uh-list)—an expert at a certain job

traveling (TRAV-uhl-ing)—moving more than one foot while holding the basketball

READ MORE

Gilliam, Mickey. *Pro Basketball Upsets*. Minneapolis: Lerner Publications, 2020.

Omoth, Tyler. *The NBA Finals*. North Mankato, MN: Capstone Press, 2019.

Slade, Suzanne. *Swish!: The Slam-Dunking, Alley-Ooping, High-Flying Harlem Globetrotters*. New York: Little, Brown and Company, 2020.

INTERNET SITES

Jr. NBA
jr.nba.com

National Basketball Association
www.nba.com

Sports Illustrated Kids
www.sikids.com

INDEX